BODYWORKS

mouth

Katherine Goode

BLACKBIRCH PRESS, INC.
WOODBRIDGE, CONNECTICUT

To Dr. Paul Goodman, with thanks

Published by Blackbirch Press, Inc.
260 Amity Road
Woodbridge, CT 06525

e-mail: staff@blackbirch.com
web site: www.blackbirch.com

Printed in Hong Kong

First published 1999 by
MACMILLAN EDUCATION AUSTRALIA PTY LTD
627 Chapel Street, South Yarra 3141

10 9 8 7 6 5 4 3 2 1

Photo Credits:
Cover photo: ©PhotoDisc
Page 1: Graham Meadows Photography; page 11: Austral International; page 28: AUSCAPE/©Y. Arthus-Bertrand-Explorer; page 23: Coo-ee Picture Library; pages 5, 14, 24, 29: Graham Meadows; pages 4, 6, 12, 17, 27: Great Southern Stock; pages 9, 22: International Photo Library; page 22: ©Ted Horowitz/Stock Photos; page 15: The Photo Library/©Omikron; pages 10, 13, 18, 19, 20, 23, 26, 30: The Picture Source.

Library of Congress Cataloging-in-Publication Data
Goode, Katherine, 1949–
Mouth / by Katherine Goode.
        p.   cm. — (Bodyworks)
    Includes index.
    Summary: Describes the functions of the different parts of the mouth.
    ISBN 1-56711-494-6 (hardcover : alk. paper)
    1. Mouth—Juvenile literature. [1. Mouth.] I. Title.
QM306.G66   2000
612.3'1—dc21
                                                                00-008315
                                                                CIP

Contents

The mouth

You use your mouth to eat, drink, and talk.

You also use your mouth when you sing and shout, and when you laugh and yawn.

The lips and cheeks

The outside parts of your mouth are the lips and cheeks. Your lips contain many small **blood vessels**. That is why they are pink and why they bleed easily.

lips   cheek

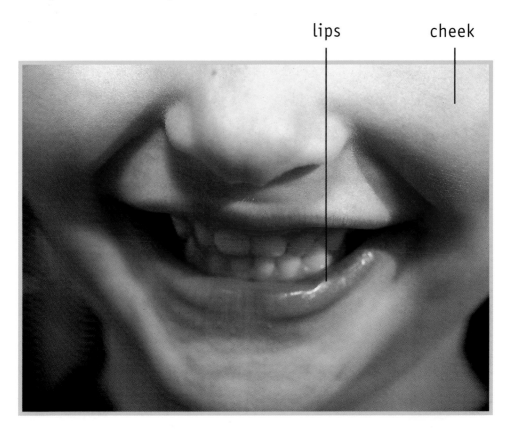

By moving your lips, you can change the shape of your mouth. You move your lips in different ways when you drink, eat, and speak.

The palate

The roof of your mouth has a bony, hard part called the hard palate. It separates your mouth and nose.

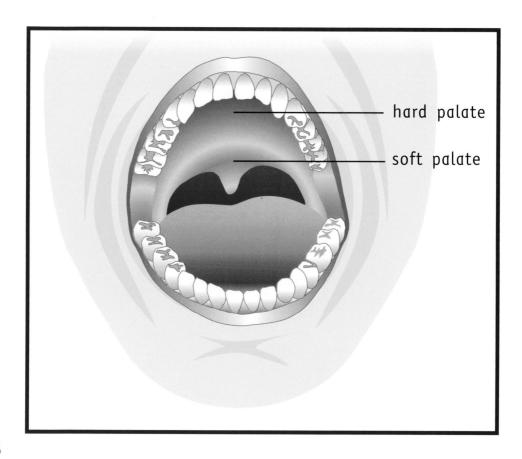

hard palate

soft palate

The soft palate hangs down between your mouth and the back of your throat. When you swallow, the soft palate closes. It stops food from entering your nose.

The tonsils

The tonsils are **tissues** on each side of the back of your mouth. When you are very young, the tonsils may help fight germs.

tonsils

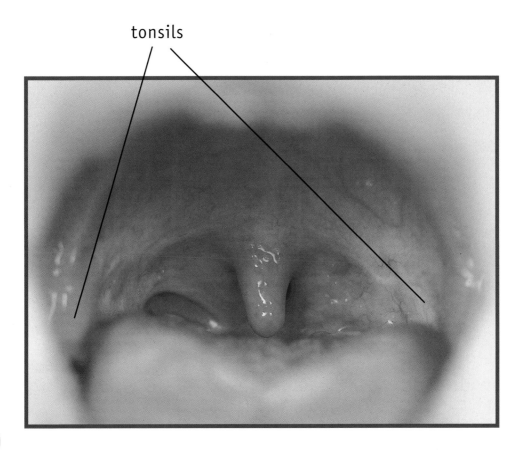

Sometimes the tonsils become red and swollen, giving you a very sore throat. If that happens, a doctor may have to remove your tonsils.

The tongue

Your tongue is made up of a group of muscles.
It is connected to the floor of your mouth.
Your tongue helps you to swallow and talk.

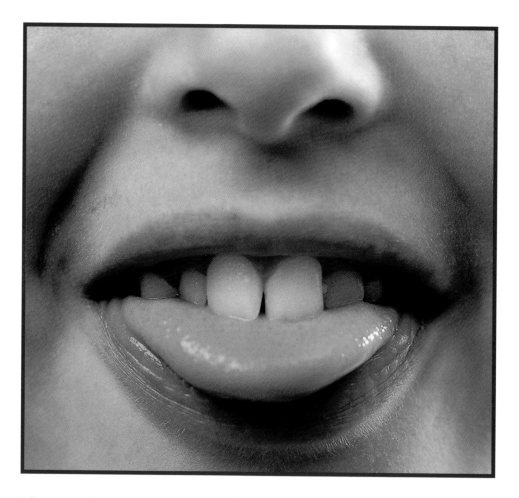

If you place your tongue between your teeth, you can make the <u>th</u> sound found in words like <u>mouth</u> and <u>teeth</u>.

You form sounds by touching the roof of your mouth and your teeth with your tongue.

Your tongue moves food around in your mouth.
It pushes the food between your upper and
lower teeth, where you chew it. Then it pushes
the food to the back of your mouth. Your
tongue helps you to swallow.

The taste buds

Your tongue contains thousands of taste buds that help you taste different kinds of food. The 4 types of taste buds are sweet, sour, salty, and bitter. You get the flavor of food by tasting and smelling it.

Close-up of a taste bud.

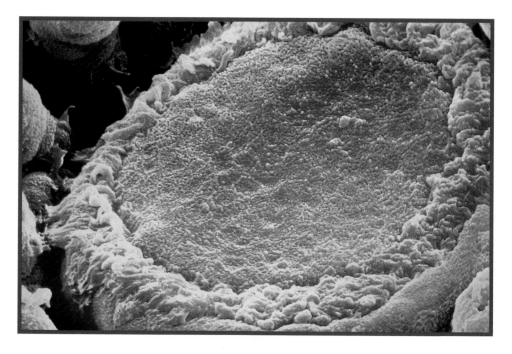

Saliva

There are **glands** in your mouth, which make a liquid called saliva. Saliva mixes with your food as you chew it.

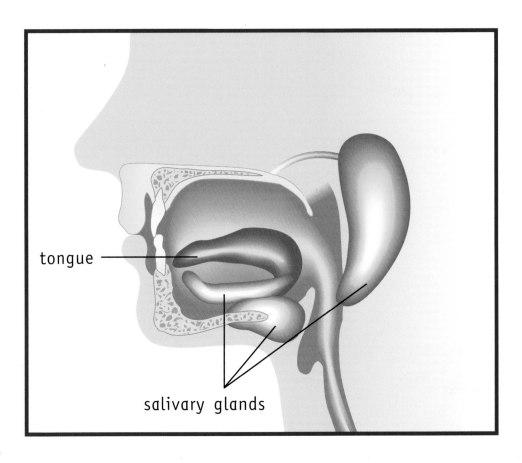

tongue

salivary glands

Saliva helps you to swallow food. After you swallow the food, it travels down to your stomach.

The jawbones

Inside your mouth are the upper and lower jawbones. The lower jaw moves up and down and is attached to your face by **muscles**. The upper jaw is part of your skull. It does not move. The jawbones contain teeth.

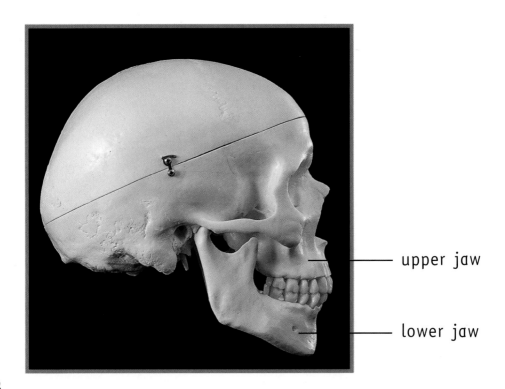

upper jaw

lower jaw

The gums

Your gums cover your jawbones. They help to hold your teeth in place. Your gums can feel pain, heat, and cold. Healthy gums are pink and tough.

gums

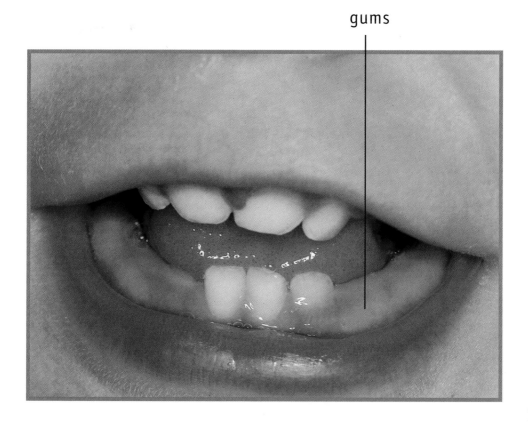

The teeth

You have an upper and lower set of teeth. Your front teeth are used for cutting food. Your back teeth grind and crush food so you can swallow it.

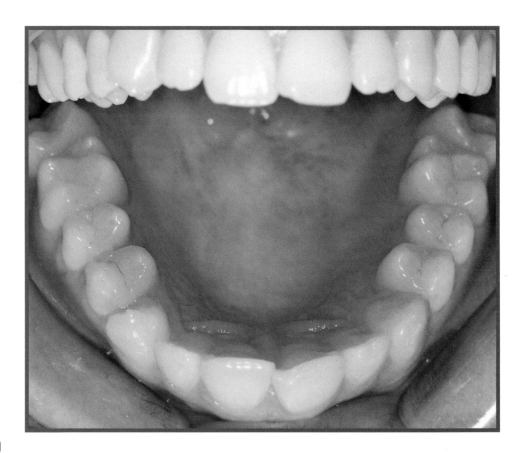

Parts of the tooth

The crown is the part of your tooth that you can see. The root is below the gum. The root holds your tooth in a **socket** in the jawbone.

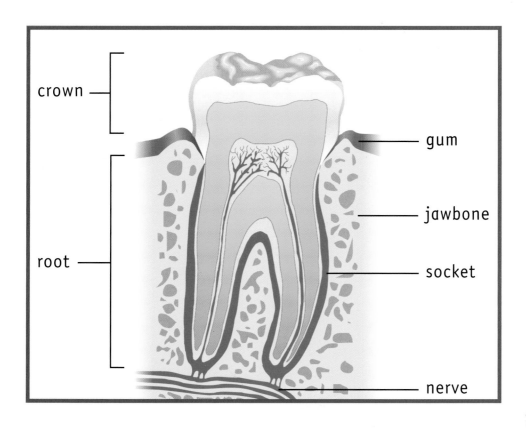

crown

root

gum

jawbone

socket

nerve

Milk teeth

You grow 2 sets of teeth in your lifetime. Your first teeth come in when you are about 6 months old. These teeth are known as milk teeth. By the time you are 2 years old, you normally have 20 milk teeth.

When you are about 3 years old, the roots of your milk teeth begin to dissolve slowly. They loosen and fall out to make room for your adult teeth.

Adult teeth

Between the ages of 6 and 12, you lose your milk teeth, and your adult teeth push through to the surface of your gums. There are 32 adult teeth.

Cavities

Cavities are holes in the teeth. Cavities form when **bacteria** in the mouth turn sugar into an acid that eats away at a tooth and forms a hole. Your dentist may coat your teeth with a special liquid that helps to prevent cavities.

cavity

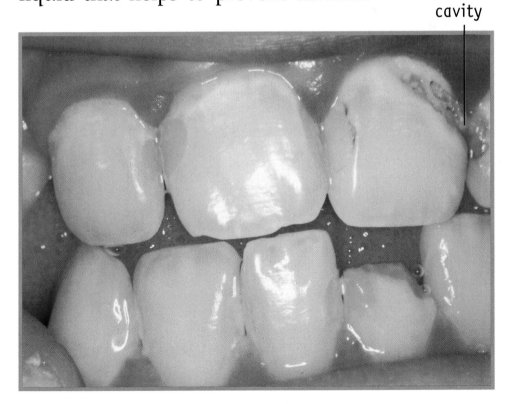

Tooth care

You should brush your teeth after every meal to protect them. You can use **dental floss** to clean the sides of your teeth and to get rid of food that gets trapped between them.

Milk, eggs, cereals, fruits, and vegetables all provide **nutrients** that help to build strong teeth. Too many sugary drinks, cakes, candy, and other sweet foods can be harmful to your teeth.

The dentist and dental assistant

Dentists and dental assistants are some of the people who care for your teeth. They clean your teeth and check them for cavities. For serious problems, special doctors are needed.

It is a good idea to visit the dentist every 6 months.

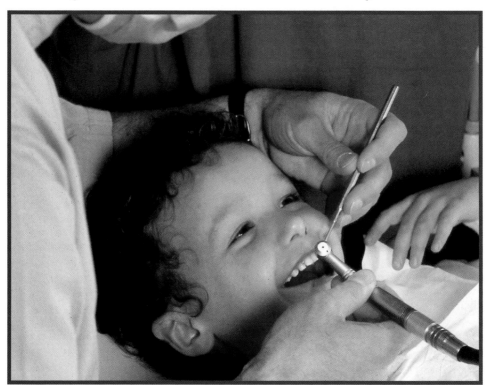

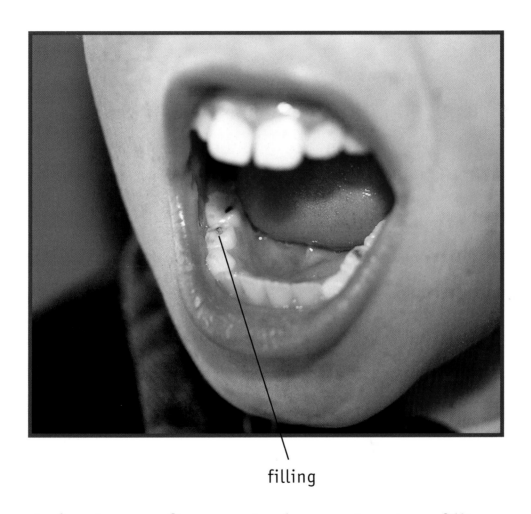

filling

A dentist can fix a cavity by putting in a filling. The dentist removes the **decayed** part of the tooth and fills the cavity with a hard material called a filling.

Braces

If your adult teeth do not fit together well, you may need braces to straighten them. Braces are bands and wires made of metal and plastic. It usually takes a few years for braces to move your teeth into the correct position.

Glossary

bacteria	germs
blood vessels	tiny tubes inside the body that carry the blood
decayed	rotten, having a cavity
dental floss	a thin piece of string that is used to clean between teeth
glands	organs of the body that produce substances for particular purposes
muscles	parts of the body that cause movement
nutrients	substances in food that are good for health
socket	a hole into which something fits
tissues	the matter that living things are made of

Index